CROWN NOBLE

CROWN NOBLE

poems by

BIANCA PHIPPS

Published by Button Poetry / Exploding Pinecone Press
Minneapolis, MN 55403 | http://www.buttonpoetry.com

LINEAGE

How can I leave without hurting
everyone that made me?

—REGINA SPEKTOR, "SMALL TOWN MOON"

. . . and nostalgia you can't trust.

—NATALIE DIAZ

CROWN NOBLE

NINA

Nina has the patience to be a pianist. She smiles to hide all her teeth. She puts her left contact in first. She lives in Seattle with her girlfriend and their rescue mutt, Harriet. Nina has a garden that draws all the neighborhood curiosity. Nina works at the elementary school teaching music. Nina is good with numbers. Nina keeps her hair short because Nina didn't braid her self-worth into its length. I mean, Nina keeps her hair short because Nina enjoys ease. Nina cries at the movies and everyone hands her a tissue. Nina has three siblings because there was no miscarriage. Nina's parents divorced with the same tenderness they used to get married. Nina is honest in therapy. Nina likes to cook for herself. Nina drinks her tea before it gets cold. Nina appreciates process. She fetches fresh vegetables twice a week. It reminds her of her father. Nina doesn't draft his eulogy. Nina calls him. Nina has a good life. Nina knows all good things must come to an end. Nina doesn't write the expiration dates in her planner. Nina likes to say goodbye. Nina has boundaries that bloom like her tulips. She embraces her lover and sleeps without dreams. Nina doesn't carry tension in her shoulders or her jaw or her bite. Nina doesn't search every room for marked exits. Nina is serene. Nina lives in the alternate world where my father won the right to name me. Nina was pulled to the clouds, and I was pressed from the clay.

FAMILY PORTRAIT, 1995

Imagine the child didn't fall far from the
metaphor. Imagine you are the apple of his
hesitation. Imagine the crown of thorns
woven from daisies. Imagine the blood of
the covenant flows thicker than the water
of the women. Imagine your family photo.
Imagine you are all smiles. Imagine the smiles
reach your eyes. Imagine your eyes. Imagine
the scramble of memory. Imagine your father's
eyes. Are they your own? Imagine the inheritance
gifted when you meet your father's eyes.
Imagine your lack of inheritance. Imagine your
father's eyes the first time he wept. Imagine how
your father clutches his sadness, christens it with
any other name. Imagine salt. Imagine a crushed
weed underfoot. Imagine a crushed parent under
fire. Imagine your father's clutched sadness;
christen it your own. Imagine the transition from
clutch to cradle. Imagine your new sadness gazes
with a stranger's eyes. Imagine the pages of the
photo album filled with proof of who belongs to
who. Imagine in every photograph your father is
blinking.

MY FATHER'S EULOGY, THE EARLY DRAFTS

we have gathered here this afternoon to celebrate

we have gathered here this afternoon to memorialize
a good man   a dear father

we have gathered here this afternoon to honor
a man we all   thought we knew

we have gathered here this afternoon to pay homage to
this man we've all met
his name was crown noble
his name was my name
          though he always prayed I would give it away
          in exchange for another man's
          but we cannot let go of what we are
          even when we bury it

we have gathered here this afternoon to remember
this man we've all met
his name is printed on the top of your program
though names are relative
                    he was something else to each of us—
                    we are only what others call us
                    when we aren't around to answer to it

we are gathered here this afternoon to remember
this man we've all met
his name is printed on the top of your program
he was something special to each of us

he is with his father now
and the Father
where he always dreamed of living
          when he dreamed of life

I cannot find it within myself to remain bitter
he did not love me enough to stay—
he is happy
now and

                isn't that all I yearned to know:

      happiness
      with my father?

REFLECTION

dad & I own the same phone case
by accident.

dad & I quote the John Mulaney stand-up
at the same time, miles apart.

dad & I drink Moscow Mules
but never together.

dad & I sing in the same off-key
& cry in the same silence.

dad & I know how to make the room laugh
so loud they forget we are there.

dad & I don't call it depression,
just the sadness, a scent to shake off

maybe soon or in death,
whichever comes last.

dad & I cradle grudges in our shoulders
against ourselves. each one is named

after the ones we've hurt—but never
our own names & never each other.

we cannot forgive what we struggle to love,
dad & I.

I mean, he loves me & I love
everyone except myself.

dad & I both call it *the sadness*,
though what we mean is

the loneliness
though what we mean is

whatever will not kill us
no matter how we beg.

A NOTE ABOUT MY FATHER

by winter break of my first year of college,
I owed $2,000 to the university and couldn't register for classes.

my father sold every piece of furniture in his house
so I could be the first person to carry our name to graduation.

love is the sacrifice and the carving knife.
guilt is the yoke that ties me to home,

and what is home but a cracked rafter
holding all the snow at bay?

THE HEARTBREAKER POEM

i.
my father spills his youth across the kitchen table:
nostalgic revelry, the color of sirens

my mother   doesn't speak

the threads that weave her tapestry
loom from my father's mouth
he unspools the way he tamed her
saved her
from a life of reckless abandonment
clipped her wings to keep her
from flying too close to the sun

but Icarus would just as soon have drowned than burned
and the silence in my mother's mouth is saltwater dark

she does not speak up to defend herself

even now, years after their divorce
my father's voice can fill a room
my mother still makes space for it

when my mother teaches me not to be swallowed
she is already sitting in the belly of the beast
i wonder if she has grown to love the cavern
like she once loved the man

ii.
the day i learn the importance of emergency exits
is the day my heartbeat stops sounding familiar
a stuttering tongue   a trembling hand

my heart beats like
closing doors

my father's fading footsteps
every plea i learn how to swallow
　　　don't *go*, don't *go*, don't *go*, don't—

my father taught me to be the first to walk away:
leave before they realize i am not worth staying for

iii.
when my mother tells me not to be afraid
of falling in love
i do not miss the way her hands shake
i wonder if they miss the handcuff weight of the ring
i wonder if i, too, will fall
in love with a padlock man

i become wary of boys with birdcage hands
their mouths like oceans
and my mother is still wringing seawater from her bones

iv.
i master the art of slipping away
by starting small:
set the body clock
　　　to keep them in the dark
plot the escape route
　　　before the entrance
force my heart to beat
　　　just *go*, just *go*, just *go*, just—

i practice on the ones i love most
solder wounds into wonder:

mangled by my hand
means safe from another's

i don't know the last time my heart
sounded like a heart

v.
he tells me, *you eat like a bird*
      i tell him, *my mother taught me well*
he laughs, and reaches for my hand
i smile, and begin to slip
through the cage
of his fingers

vi.
when the boys begin the hunt
for fabled bedroom healers
i warn them:
broken glass bottled shipwreck interior
no room for mending

they don't care   or   they don't hear me

they cut themselves on sharp tongues
make finger paintings with blood on their hands
a soft pastel shimmer image that looks so much like me
i almost believe it a mirror

                        almost

soon
they will wake with scars and blame me

i leave them a bandage in the dark and don't look back
i leave before they realize i am not worth scarring for

vii.
every outstretched hand   wants me drowned

i sink further underwater
ignore the burning in my chest
run my fingers over the names
leaving my mouth
for the last time
and convince myself
this is the victory

CROWN REGENT

Mother is here, too. A siren who traded her fins for legs. A champion runner. Could have been a bird. Was a student in dental school. Wanted to be a ballerina. A point guard. A disco ball. I follow Mother into all the club bathrooms & meet her eyes in the mirror. Neither of us know how to go home. Mother is a flashing light. A tinny voice on the other end of the phone. Mother has agency. Mother makes her own choices. Is golden yarn. Was spun to save someone else. Mother used to sneak out of her own window. Mother never stopped. Mother made windows out of people. Mother is afraid I'll turn into a mother. Mother is afraid I'll turn. Mother is afraid of my reflection in her mirror. Mother is proud of me. Mother made her own choices. Mother is out there, somewhere, dancing. Mother is a good skater. Mother is a good runner. Mother is a good tennis player. Mother is a good mother. Mother never lies but I do.

ESTRELLA

mom never talked much about the day she met dad
& that was alright with me because i didn't have much
to ask. i mean, i had already written the story in my head:

my mother, young,
dressed in the polyester skirt
that made her feel faster
& skates painted from tongue to tip
with the delicacy of a butcher's hand.
tied with the laces she lifted from the payless
four backyards from her front door.
a smear of gold against the wooden walls of the roller rink.
my father, a shadow
billowed in the corner to smoke
with friends & skates kept powder white
through the luxury of time.
he rolled into the rink to race & found a comet
stole his spot. she was speed. untouchable.
gold hoops and a laugh so loud
it lasted until i was born.
she slowed down
enough to make my father a starcatcher
& then he was in orbit.
my father's year around the rink
was an hour out of my mother's day.
it was the last time she was fast enough
to outrun him.

IT JUST HAPPENED SO FAST

One minute everyone clambered onto the same couch
& the next we didn't.
Or is that just memory? Anyway,
I betrayed them. I told Dad
where we were going. I thought they loved each other.
I loved them both. I couldn't imagine a world
where they didn't—love each other like I loved them.
I could forgive them for anything.
It all changed. But it was me:
I unlocked the door
& left a note
& told him where we were going.
I wanted him to follow.
My fault. My love.
My inability to separate them.

BORN TO EMBODY IT

"My wound existed before; I was born to embody it."

—JOË BOUSQUET

my body has never been mine
alone

always a shared space
with the ghosts of my father's past
and my mother's favorite demons
and little room for me.

I am a product of my mother's fragile vertebrae
and my father's miserable veins

an attempt at creation by two bodies
designed for destruction
insatiable need to feel something
no matter the cost.

my father tells me of the monster
hidden underneath my skin
on a Wednesday afternoon.

he christens it *addiction.*

he speaks of its ways
with the tone one would use
to describe a lover that scorned them:
with anger, with adoration.
the way he speaks of my mother.

he tells me how it rattles our fault-line bones
tells me it rots our family tree
too fast for any branch to escape.
I can't tell if this is an apology.

this means, he tells me,
that we will never know how to let go.

we will cling to something until it chokes us
we will let it, we will love it.

he says this like a warning
but it sounds like his wedding vows:

I will love you until it kills me
and then I will love you more.

I was born to a pair of addicts
desperate for each other
a fire that consumed them whole—

I am my father's daughter   my mother's mirror
designed to seek that which can destroy me
and let it, and love it

I was carved hollow by hands that loved me
to hold wars in the spaces between my ribs
to see destruction written across my fingertips

I am clockwork catastrophe catalyst
a girl of ash and broken glass
the remnants of a Molotov cocktail marriage
I was born to go up in flames

a can of gasoline in love with a match
I would let myself burn just to feel warm.

                I am scared I have sought you out:
                  I am a doused woman drowning
                    you are frayed electricity
                      dressed as a lifeline.

                  you could tear me to pieces

                    and I would let you.
                      and love you.

STICK

you split me like a shell in your teeth, spit out the hard interior.
giggling is a fool's feeling and i am a fool around you. all laugh.
face split, cheeks ache, you make me smile like an eggshell crack.
my capillaries want to move into your lungs. could you make room?
is there a vacancy i can fill with my gallbladder? can you host my
heartbeat in the place beneath your ear? it is my favorite place.
my thighs would love to meet with your hips, if you have the time.
each molar whispers about you to my gums. my tongue runs over
to soothe them into silence, but it doesn't last. could your kidneys
pencil mine in for coffee? my ankles crack up near you. you send
them rolling. can you see? my eyes are nervous, can't make contact.
my hair sticks to your sweatshirt. wants to curl with you.
if you'd have me, i'd come over. we could make a good mess.

MOONSTRUCK

jumping spiders can see the moon
& i wonder if they jump to get closer.
when the spiders teach me how to speak,
i want them to start with the word *moon*.
i want to know if it sounds anything like
my word for *yearn*, which is spelled like
your name while you sleep in our bed.
jumping spiders have eyes like telescopes,
able to see without turning their heads.
what is the spider word for *telescope*?
is it just *eye*? what is the spider word
for what i am? where you are? do the
spiders have a word for *home*, and is it
spelled like *distance*? i watched a spider
try to hitch a ride on the van's antenna
& i thought about the spider word for
fear. must be close to their word for *love*.
i, too, would fling myself across the country
or the street to get where i needed to go.
needed to go here might be *moon* or *love*
or our bed before you wake up without me
again. god knows i am grateful we share
the moon if we cannot share a bed. the
spiders may not have a word for *jump*. i
may not have a word for how i do not think
to love you; i simply blink & there you are:
my underbelly, my tender place. it is just
how we exist. they *jump*. i *love*. and we
all stare up at the moon.

ALMOSTS

I have never felt so at ease
as I did the day you called me precocious.

> I have never feared big words,
> only those that refused to use them,
> and the syllables rolled off your tongue like honey—
> I was hooked.

Language became ours.
> (And I know that everybody uses language,
> but this was different,
> as if in between the letters
> and the syllables
> there was a secret message
> only we could decipher.)

My days filled with the sound of your voice,
and your nights became littered with the loops of my handwriting.

We exchanged our favorite words:
> mine: *illuminated,*
> yours: *catawampus,*
and our least favorites:
> mine: *moist,*
> and yours:
> *almost.*

When I asked you why,
you said it was because almost held failed potential,
> represented our ability to be just not good enough.
> We came to the brink of something beautiful
> and fell short so many times
> > we crafted a word for it.

But even we, with our supposed mastery of English,
        were not invulnerable to our shortcomings.

Words only help if you speak them.

I never told you I loved you.
You never told me you were dying.

Five words each:

I love you, I think.
                              I have a brain tumor.

To this day I don't know all the details;
medical jargon never fit in my mouth
and even now it feels like an invasion of your privacy,

        but I have pored over our conversations
        searching for the secret message,

and I am sorry,
but I only almost found it.

        Saltwater is not good for paper.
        My tears warped your words.

After some serious consideration,
I've decided to change my least favorite word,
because while *moist* is gross,
                    malignant is malicious.
                    Malignant is uncontrollable,
                    means a phone call and the phrase
                        he didn't wake up.
                    Malignant is messy, unfair, a thief.
                    Malignant means I never got to say goodbye.
                    Malignant is the cause of almost.

You were on the brink of something beautiful,
but you couldn't quite reach it,
and you fell too far.
I am so sorry I wasn't there to catch you.

I hope your heaven is a library.
I hope it is void of *almosts*.

Te amo, Daniel.
Sleep well.

I AM ALL THE ROOTS

i am swathed in the luxury of wanting—
how it maroons me & blues me & crushes me.

underneath: a verdant biodome. i unfurl in the humidity,
flytrap eyelids with radiant curl & radiant teeth,

hibiscus bloom cheeks, clipped bush mouth, all roots
running under skin. it's all beauty, really, run by fear.

root veins drink at the feet of anxious electricity.
i drip lush negativity. i dress in pretend forgetfulness.

i want to be a greenhouse. i want to be a devourer. i want
& it gives me away. i want to be a terrifying unknown

& i want to be loved. i always pick love. i can't help it.
i suck at the root of love. i drink at Their feet. i want Them

to pick me & i let Them dress me in green. it brings out
the color of me. the color they like. i pretend to be a girl

They will be proud of. i want to be grateful so i write
myself into a garden & let them prune me & harvest.

but: i did not forget. i am flourish & flesh. i, heartbeat.
i, want & wanted. worthy outside expectations. i suck

at the root of love & am nourished. i am all the roots, remember?
i am the humidity bloom. i, love & loved. i am afraid & still

i live. i live. I live.

IN THE CLOUDS

Nina and her mother sit across from each other at the kitchen table and clip coupons. Nina and her mother tuck their hair behind their ears at the same time but neither notices. Nina looks up a moment too late. Nina studies her mother. Nina's mother is gray around the edges. Nina's mother doesn't dye her hair; Nina's mother doesn't fear the mirror. Nina studies the wrinkles between her mother's brows, charts the terrain of peaks and valleys. Nina is the cartographer of her future. Nina's mother leans back in her chair and the space between her brows smooths into a lake. Nina's mother smiles at her daughter's curiosity. Nina looks to the scissors in her left hand. Nina gathers courage from the coupon in her right. Nina admires the careful boundary the dotted lines create. Nina says to the coupon, the room, the future: *I like girls, too*. Nina cuts the boundary. Nina's mother sets her scissors on the table. Nina suffers in the silence. Nina's mother extends her hand across the table and lifts her former chin. Nina cries. Nina's life is full of water. Nina's mother says, *Okay*. Nina and her mother smile at the same time. *That's okay.*

ELENA ALVAREZ IS LIVING MY BEST LIFE

& I mean it / with a sincerity that overwhelms me / I mean
when I watch her / I look into a mirror & want / to care for what
I see / for the first time / I see what I could have been / had I
found the girl earlier / or / had a mom like Penelope / instead /
I observe from my couch / ache for a life I never got / but almost
had / Penelope praises Elena / for stealing hotel toiletries / & I
am fourteen again / flushed with pride at my miniature haul /
and my mom cooed / I learned to love hungry / learned nothing
/ in the pantry was the sure way to beautiful / I was only six
empty stomachs away / from being her perfect girl / she taught
me / men will ruin your life / she didn't mention girls / neither
did I / couldn't tell her I wanted to kiss / my friends / want / is
what keeps us from perfection / shame is our love language /
guilt / the mother's tongue / Penelope confesses to Elena / we all
cry / in the car ride home / from planned parenthood / my mom
confesses to me / she had a bad mom too / and it was the closest
we ever got / to apology

SONNET FOR MY DAUGHTER

from my mother to me

i dreamt of the lives that could have been mine
       (dressmaker, horticulturist, doula,
       ethical hacker, hotel manager,
       perfumist, pilot, a bounty hunter,
       locomotive engineer, stunt double,
       dentist, sommelier, ocularist)
while cradling the swollen belly that locked
all doors but one. my identity was
relative now. you made me mother and
stole all the rest. gilded cagemate, child:
you lock-picked your way into the world and
left nothing for me to eat. i starved, so
i fled. you'll understand when you're older:
we only get one chance to escape love.

LENGUA

we're all screaming as we play loteria
& jack wins again with la bota. we
laugh & it almost sounds like a family.
mom laughs the loudest. mom always
laughs the loudest & it's always so
quiet when she's gone & it's always quiet.

> everybody tells me i look like my mom
> except my mom who says i look like
> my dad. we both know what it means.

the tias talk shit about me at christmas
in spanish & i smile while they do it.
i don't defend myself. i probably deserve it.
wouldn't know. i got the wrong tongue;
i got all the names for what's wrong
with us but only in ingles, so.

> i'm not my grandmother's favorite grandchild
> but we are the most alike. nobody likes me
> because i am a reflection.

dad always talked about what grandma conjured.
once in the night they all heard a scream
that drove him & his siblings & his parents
into the hallway. the story goes nobody was there
but the family, exposed in their fear.

> we don't talk about the screams in the night
> that drive us out of our rooms. we're not
> supposed to give it the power of a name.

the truth is i look like both my parents but
they don't look at me. i want to talk about
the screaming. the absence in the hallway
of something else to blame. i want to talk
& i got the wrong tongue & it conjures all
we look away from when the light turns on.

THE SNOW CONVINCED THE PLANE TO STAY HOME

for one more night. The plane agreed,
and we all stayed for one more night, too.
Our entire neighborhood remembered the
joy of *snow day*. We walked to Seth's as
children threw soft fistfuls at their siblings
and their parents watched, soothed for now.
The journey back home was treacherous. The
full case of PBR was passed back and forth
as we took turns throwing snow. It was your
burden and you set it down, asked me to wait
with you. Our band of friends moved ahead
and you kissed me. I forgot about our friends,
the children, the people at the airport. I forgot
about the morning that loomed over me, about
Christmas at home. I forgot we had not spent
our entire lives kissing. It was as new then as
it is now. You kissed me as the world froze.
Come on, you said, snow crowding your hair
to get a better look. *We've got all night.*

WHEN THE BOY SAYS HE LOVES MY BODY

but does not say he loves me,
      I let him.

I close my eyes
      and feel his matchstick fingers
      strike against my skin.

I feel how he burns the girl out of flesh,
      sucks the blue out of bones,
      admires the glass jar
      that traps the dying firefly.

How pretty, the frame.
How soft, the entrance.
How beautiful, the archway
      that gapes into the burned-out church.

When he leaves, his arsonist hands
flick a final spark into my mouth
      so I remember how he feels,
      so I think him when I think myself,
      so I write his name in whatever is left.
I find my body is a locked door.
I find I locked myself out.
I find I did it on purpose.

If the boy will love the body
      and burn the girl,
      she will learn to make a home upwind of ash
      and pretend she is not cold.

Suddenly everything is the body.
The weight.
      The worth.
            The shape.
                 The case.

It is easier to pretend   the girl never existed,
that all there ever was
was flesh, and cartilage, and blood—

If I pretend I never learned to kiss the ground and call it lover,
I never buried myself under the carcass of everything I used to trust.
Nothing went wrong.
I laugh along with the song of my own undoing.
Never tell anyone how I forgot to go home.
        How I couldn't.
        How I don't know where I left the key.

I became a stranger in the window,
the ghost in the eaves.
The body became haunted,
mausoleum,
burnt sea.

I forgot to forgive what could not ask for forgiveness.
I forgot it was not what needed forgiving.

The body cries for me to come home,
        and I only hear his voice
        asking with what tender touch
        I would like to be evicted.

If I go back,
        what will be left?

What does the forest lose before it trusts the sun again?
What does it cost to reach for warmth and mistake it for war?
How does it unlearn the fear of beauty, wildness, becoming a
    target?
Will I ever cease building myself into a castle of kindling?

Does the firefly hate the hands that trapped it
        or the glass jar it died inside?

Does it live long enough to choose?

STAY WITH ME

talking is a matter of convincing my tangled mouth to create
something coherent, but it only works *sometimes* I don't know
what to say *next* time I see you I will be *honest* to God I'm trying
I *promise* you won't walk out before you wake me, I *wouldn't* it
be nice if I could keep the same line of *thoughts* are wreckage,
they scatter, they're *everywhere* I go I return to the time I allowed
that boy to confess he loved me though I knew he was *lying* next to
you is the quietest my mind has ever been. the howls and
hisses smooth into a chorus of tamed, holy beasts. the constriction
thaws, I break free, I breathe. I breathe. I breathe to reveal this
to you, but I worry it will ruin *everything* happens for a reason
yet I couldn't tell you the reason behind that *choice* is difficult
with anxiety, I struggle to identify the lesser of two precipices
and therein lies the *danger* is the familiar taste of a rainslick
unlit side street, keys crowded in between the knuckles of my
stronger *hand* him my secrets and give his earthquake fingers a
loaded gun to press against my *heart* beats: the body's language
of choice. a thousand silent signals passed from my wrist to
yours. I wonder what my skin has been able to communicate
and if any of it will be the right *one* day I'll tame this wild
garden mouth and cultivate something *soft* does not mean
weak; it means *gentle* men with sharp teeth know to draw blood
without *notice* me, please, I'm *right here* is every ghost I haven't
learned to let go *of* everything I've lost, all I want back is *time*
has a gift for warping the memory of warmth, clouding what
you used to *remember* the first time I cried? my body shook
apart. your hands wove the steady net. I spilt sorry like an
accident. a cut tongue. the safest way to see you out. you didn't
go. I've stopped waiting for you to. trust, I'm learning, is not a
soft gift, but worth the pain. somewhere in this coward mouth
is a brave heart's confession. please tell me you hear it. I can't
promise how long this clarity will *last* time I visited home, my
dad asked why I wouldn't date anyone, so I lied: no one interested
me *enough* men have left with scraps of me between their teeth
that I can't remember the taste of feeling *whole* armies have

fallen to poor planning; my mouth stumbles to keep me from *falling* in secret is the loveliest form of *self-destruction* is two people who drown warning signs under the sheets and ignore the way it screams *no* person ever asked me for details of what he *did* I lose you?

FLYPAPER

in summer
the spiders haunt every underpass:
doorways, stairs beneath the train, streetlamps

i skitter underneath
nervous blood flaps my wings faster
as i fly through the gaps in their webs

i know it's silly to be afraid of what can only hurt me
if i am foolish enough to get caught
                                        still
i don't breathe until i am inside
                my skin crawls with phantom legs
                        a learned response

in childhood
my home was planted on the edge of a southern forest
my bedroom window turned my room lighthouse
summoned all the underbrush crawlers to nest inside

i left the window open in mid-july
the scent of my sleep sweat sung across the wood
an invitation i didn't know i handed out

i woke to find i'd been invaded
the second story security
                scattered   scuttled
along the walls   the floor   the bed
nothing mine but my scream wide mouth eyes shut

                and my parents ran in
                swore it was all a dream

i knew they were wrong
and that they must be right:

if i had not dreamed it
it would become another shedskindust
to sweep under the rug
so i—dutiful daughter despite the damage—
let it slink out of the room
this shadow i could never name again

until

in adolescence
i'd grown older by a fistful of months
and a few familial fractures
        living in a selfish house with
        no room for our growing bodies

i left the door open
        a memory of fresh air
the hall light like the moon
        a warm, dim glow
slung across the wooden slats
        to the foot of my bed

there is an animal part of us that thrives on instinct:

some feral ghost   trapped in sinew
follows the light   finds a bone to suck dry
sucks the bone dry   uncovers a feast
some of our ghosts   are the feast
the bloody wreckage   left behind

everything glows in amber:
i remember no sharp teeth
            no dirt under my nails
            no soft lullaby of smothering

i remember what has no name:

the feeling of hands like bugs like fingers like
          crawling like
     a touch can steal my breath in all the wrong ways

i did not scream. i remembered that much.
when they came, the room would be empty
and my body would be hollow

and they'd shake their heads and say   a dream

a dream with hands like eyes like
a boy with my blood and yet none of it like
a bug sucks blood and knows nothing else like
i left the door open, so.

          i slept on top of the covers, so.
          i had this dream before, so.
          a dream can't hurt you if you're still, so.

i closed my eyes. waited for everything to end.

felt my skin crawl away with him
               that good ghost dribbled out of his hungry
                    hands.

in time
these old dreams like unseen cobwebs
     startle me back to the past.
melt into one swampy puddle, slip through my fingers.
i mix the bugs with the boy until they are one:
     thorax against my thigh. antennae over my stomach.

his mouth opens to whisper he's sorry
and a thousand slugs fall out.

A RHYTHM A PATTERN

the language of history
is blood

& mine raves in the streets
a seized capillary pulsing

the inherited panic
bathes in my aorta

what is history if not
a vein that pumps from

the heart
of where you come from

& who brought you
into today

& who leaves you
made better or worse

guilt is the heartsong
i will sing at my funeral

i am the ventricle
through which it all flows

never the daughter or sister or girl
but the hollow

through which everything falls
apart

ANOTHER NOTE ABOUT MY FATHER

spring semester of my sophomore year of college
my father told me without my love, he would kill himself.

I have always been the confessional booth &
the silent deity on the other side.

guilt, the noose that ties me to home.
he slips his head in the loop & tosses me the other end.

when I try to leave
we will all come swinging down.

THE DREAM

after Felix Pollack

I dreamt of my brother disappearing and returning as a doll.
Guilt, said my therapist.
You should call home more, said my father.
Grief is a twisted comfort, said my love.
You miss him as a child, said my therapist.
The phone works both ways, I said to my father's voicemail.
You hold a lot of love in your heart and it curdles
because you leave it there, said the fog.
I dreamt he disappeared & what I meant is he died
& they gave me a doll to mourn over, I said.
Guilt twists itself into grief, said my therapist.
Who would you be without your mourning? said the fog.
Everyone always dreams about me
doing what they don't want me to do, said my brother.
I don't want you to die, I said.
But then I won't grow older, he said. *Then I'll be young forever.*
We all dream of dying, said my father.
We don't always get to follow our dreams, said the fog.
I just wanted to fly, said my brother. *You'll always see me in the*
    mourning.

SURVIVOR'S WEIGHT

all the small boys on the street
look like my brothers. all the
small boys are sunkissed. they
eat joy. their freckles spell my
name and my freckles spell theirs.
all the small boys are my brothers.
I walk away from them. all the
small boys are my brothers. they're
all strangers. a small brown boy
jumped in front of the bullets to
protect his classmates and I avoid
all the videos. I am a coward and
all the small brown boys are dying.
when we were placed in foster care
they took Jack from me. put him in
a different home. he would be down
the road, they said to me. he'll be
safe and you can be a child. it was
all foreign to me. like he is. I love all
the small boys on the street because
they don't know how I hurt them. I
love my brothers more than I hate
myself and that's why I didn't run
away when I had the chance. I waited
until it wasn't running away. it was
going to college. a small brown boy
jumped in front of the bullets and
now he doesn't get to go to college.
I wanted to be that child and now
my brothers aren't going to college.
we don't all get to choose how we
escape but I did. all I regret is that
I don't regret my choice enough.

CROWN GARLAND

when i found out steven was in jail

(steven is my brother. the middle child.
the boy i raised. the boy i fed. the boy
with a feral laugh and a homesick cry.
steven is a piece of my soul. my brother—
my child. i was a child when i raised him:
children raising children. then i left.

i left. each thought backward threatened
to turn me salt. threatened to turn me
stone. threatened to send him back to hell.
it could be any myth. he and i both know
the tender way a knife slides out of muscle
like a person slides out of the house at night.
blood comes from the holding and we never
grasped how to unfurl our fists.

pride clouds my throat like a bone. i am
left to choke on curdled apologies. i
sound selfish, and it's because i am. i
could never love him more than myself.
steven, i apologize too late. i come
home and the locks have been changed
and the children have been changed, too.

steven, my soul was splintered long ago
and the cracks have filled with guilt. it
looks like old smiles and the first summer
you ran away. sorry i didn't look longer.
sorry i stopped looking at all. my eyes
aren't closed anymore. i keep calling
olly olly oxen free. it's getting dark.
you can come home now. it's safe. you're
safe.)

i waited two days to cry.

CLOUDMOTHER

Nina doesn't dream of motherhood. Nina doesn't have anything to prove. Nina doesn't run her tongue over inherited trauma. Nina is not afraid of what rattles in her brain. She knows the names of the plagues. Names are the difference between cured and curdled. Nina knows this. Nina finds power in the names. Nina knows what is hereditary and what can be cleansed with attention. Nina is a master of attention. Nina doesn't imagine the ways a child could be ruined: a bloody birth, the argument that breaks the dishes, words as sharp as the slap, mornings coated in slick smoke, a fist that impresses the wall, a stray comment, a stray bullet, a bullet on target, curdled love, herself, the wrong babysitter, the wrong choice, the wrong name. Nina doesn't dwell on fear. Nina doesn't dwell on wonder. Nina is not afraid. Nina doesn't think parenting requires a prerequisite. Nina thinks she could be a good parent and the thought alone satisfies. Nina has never felt unequipped. Really, Nina isn't afraid of herself. Really, that's all it takes.

PRO-CHOICE

i was unwanted.

my first name was
how could you do this to me?

they love me now, yes.
doesn't alleviate the sting.

sometimes, i'm mean
to the people that love me
because i know i'm not
supposed to be here.

i took this life
from her.
whoever my mother
could have been

if she'd had a choice.

WHITE RIVER WRITES HOME

I love you. I used to want it simpler, yet
I am of your mold. The fact of love is all it takes.

Like you, I worry what you'd think of me
if you knew the whole truth. Dad, I am just a girl:

clove and cinnamon, two clasped daisies,
a load-bearing responsibility. I know you

love me, Dad, and I know the parts of me
you hate. Daughter is not enough context

to cover it all. I don't keep you at an arm's
length because of your heart. It's mine.

My heart is a messy liar. The silence between
us shoves everything under the bed. A clean

room hides my iridescent heart. A stunted
tongue stutters blood over the past and becomes

the truth to everyone who wasn't there.
A metaphor blurs the face of who you call

daughter even when she doesn't call you.
I want you to love me and I want to be the

sole bearer of truth. The two are only aligned
in silence. So I was quiet. I need to be loud now,

Dad. I need my love to gleam in the sunlight.
I used to dream we remained as ghosts.

We haunted a new family and never talked
about our own. We ached for the sun. Love

doesn't belong to ghosts, Dad. Love belongs
to the living. I am alive, Dad. I tended to the blooms

I watched you cut at the root. Here is the sun:
I could love a woman like I love my man.

I'd want you to love her like you love me:
honest, unquestioned, shameless. But you can't

if you don't know. Now you know. You were
always afraid I'd never be able to love. You

worried you had scratched that part of my heart
to dirt. Love is alive in me, Dad. I love myself,

Dad. You could give up on me now and I
wouldn't starve. But I'd never be full.

Forgiveness is not a relentless feast. It is a slow
turn toward the light. I ask shame to leave

and reverse its mantras:
I am good.

No parts of me are broken.
I am not a shattered mirror.

I am a human with a great capacity for delight.
I am loved and become love in return.

I forgive myself
and, always, myself is also you.

MY FATHER'S EULOGY, EDITED

we are   here   to celebrate

a good   father

we   gathered here   to honor

his name

        he always wanted me to

                remember

his name

        he was something

           special

he

      always dreamed of living

he did   love me

&

isn't that all I yearned to know

?

NINA REDUX

Nina doesn't practice the piano. Nina doesn't eat sweet potatoes. Nina doesn't kiss her girlfriend in secret or in public or at all. Nina doesn't know the taste of her brother's cooking. Nina doesn't praise her father's success. Nina doesn't cherish the melody of her mother's true laugh. Nina doesn't craft her children's middle names. Nina doesn't clip coupons, doesn't tend to the tulips, doesn't walk Harriet twice a day. Nina doesn't learn forgiveness is not a metaphor but an eternal gift. Nina doesn't have the walks to Blockbuster. Nina doesn't have the drive to Disney World. Nina doesn't press the good memories for preservation. Nina doesn't learn sacrifice is the seed of gratitude. Nina doesn't learn that survival is the sprout of everyone that cried before. Nina doesn't carry her mother's trauma in her locket, her father's grief in her wallet. Nina doesn't carry her parents' love in her spine. Nina can't celebrate her brothers' victory. Nina can't call home, call back, call forth. Nina can't live. Nina is the handcrafted portrait of the southern woods at dusk, and I am the view through the window: in motion, untouchable, drenched in the sun.

ACKNOWLEDGMENTS

I have an immense amount of gratitude to these publications for housing the following poems, some in different forms:

Electric Moon Magazine: "I Am All the Roots"
indicia: "Flypaper"
Blue River Review: "Family Portrait, 1995"

I am so incredibly thankful to Button Poetry for believing in this book and me.

Thank you to the folks who read the early drafts of this manuscript. You helped me shape these scribblings into a coherent exploration of self: Hanif Abdurraqib, Safia Elhillo, Kevin Kantor, Sienna Burnett, Emryse Geye, Devin Devine, Madeline Lessing.

I'm eternally grateful to the artists that I have learned from, some of whom I am lucky enough to call my friends. I have gleaned and hoarded and cherished everything you have gifted me: Bernard Ferguson, Daniela Aguilar, Gina Conto, Spencer Althoff, Grace Hutchings, Alina Burgos, Hannah Carmichael, Adrienne Novy, Caroline M. Watson, Teagan Walsh-Davis, Felix Mayes, Dru Smith, Rashaad Hall, Ken Arkind, Carrie Rudzinski, Isaac Gomez, Jesse Parent, Billy Tuggle, Hannah Clark, Sarah Brown, Katie Becker Colón, Ezra Colón, Matthew Olson, Sarah Adler, Jessie Ellingsen, Hieu Ngyuen, Dylan Garity, Neil Hilborn, Madison Mae Parker, Hilary Williams, Spencer Huffman, and countless others.

Thank you to my internet friends: Alethea, Sondra, Lydia, Molly, Lauren, Kelsey, Sarah, Aliera, Dree, Daniel, the rest—Alice and I are always indebted to you. Thank you for giving me a safe place to grow.

I want to thank Opera House, Friendship Ave, all three CUPSI teams. I would have never made it out of college alive if it weren't for your constant companionship, love, tenacity.

Thank you to the 22nd class. #48hands

Thank you to Chris Stewart and Maya Garcia. You have never given up on me and I will never give up on you.

I want to say thank you to the educators that got me here, and specifically to Brian Eanes. I think everyone in the world needs an educator like you. You were my first champion. I'll never be able to repay you.

I want to thank you, Sam. I trust you. I love you. Thank you for everything.

I want to thank my family. It takes a village, and mine is the best. Mom, Dad, Steven, Jack: I love you. It is as simple and complex as that. You helped shape me into the person I've become. I love her, and I love you.

Thank you, reader, for picking this book out of thousands and making it this far.

ABOUT THE AUTHOR

Bianca Phipps (she/her) is a queer Latinx poet, actor, and teaching artist raised in San Antonio, Texas. Her work has been featured in different mediums and in different places, including Button Poetry, *Blue River Review*, *Electric Moon Magazine*, *indicia*, *Persephone's Daughters*, and others. Phipps' theatrical credits include *Romeo & Juliet*, *Othello*, *Julius Caesar* (Nebraska Shakespeare), *Hamlet* (Midsommer Flight), *I Am Not Your Perfect Mexican Daughter* (u/s, Steppenwolf), *Welcome to Keene, New Hampshire* (Strawdog Theater), and others. She is an Aquarius, an Enneagram 2, and a Slytherin. She currently lives in Chicago.

Twitter: @biancajphipps
Instagram: @biancaphipps

OTHER BOOKS BY BUTTON POETRY

If you enjoyed this book, please consider checking out some of our others, below. Readers like you allow us to keep broadcasting and publishing. Thank you!

Neil Hilborn, *Our Numbered Days*
Hanif Abdurraqib, *The Crown Ain't Worth Much*
Sabrina Benaim, *Depression & Other Magic Tricks*
Rudy Francisco, *Helium*
Rachel Wiley, *Nothing Is Okay*
Neil Hilborn, *The Future*
Phil Kaye, *Date & Time*
Andrea Gibson, *Lord of the Butterflies*
Blythe Baird, *If My Body Could Speak*
Desireé Dallagiacomo, *SINK*
Dave Harris, *Patricide*
Michael Lee, *The Only Worlds We Know*
Raych Jackson, *Even the Saints Audition*
Brenna Twohy, *Swallowtail*
Porsha Olayiwola, *i shimmer sometimes, too*
Jared Singer, *Forgive Yourself These Tiny Acts of Self-Destruction*
Adam Falkner, *The Willies*
Kerrin McCadden, *Keep This To Yourself*
George Abraham, *Birthright*
Omar Holmon, *We Were All Someone Else Yesterday*
Rachel Wiley, *Fat Girl Finishing School*
Nava EtShalom, *Fortunately*

Available at buttonpoetry.com/shop and more!